nature's
baby animals

BABY ANIMALS
OF THE GRASSLANDS

Carmen Bredeson

Dennis L. Claussen, Ph.D., *Series Science Consultant* Professor of Zoology, Miami University, Oxford, Ohio

Allan A. De Fina, Ph.D., *Series Literacy Consultant* Past President of the New Jersey Reading Association, Chairperson, Department of Literacy Education, New Jersey City University, Jersey City, New Jersey

CONTENTS

ENDANGERED
ANIMAL OF THE
GRASSLANDS

WORDS TO KNOW

endangered (ehn DAYN jurd) A type of animal that is in danger of disappearing from the earth forever.

pouch (powch) A sac used to hold something.

prey (pray) An animal that is food for another animal.

tusk (tuhsk) A long tooth that sticks out of an animal's mouth.

WHERE ARE GRASSLANDS?

3

■ = GRASSLANDS

GRASSLANDS

Grasslands are covered with grasses.

There are not many trees or bushes.

Animals have few places to hide.

Baby animals have special ways to

stay safe and live in the grasslands.

5

BABY **OSTRICH**

Ostrich eggs are the biggest eggs in the world! The chicks hatch with feathers the color of dirt. This makes it easier to hide from enemies. An ostrich cannot fly, but it can run very, very FAST on its long legs.

Baby lions are called cubs. Their mother hides them in tall grass to keep them safe. Soon they will learn to hunt for **prey** like zebras and wild pigs. Lions see very well at night. That is when they usually look for food.

BABY LION

A baby bison is called a calf.

BABY BISON

A bison calf stays close to its mother.
The calf has red hair when it is little.
As the calf grows, its hair gets darker.
Long, thick hair keeps the bison warm
during the cold winter months.

A baby kangaroo is the size of a jelly bean when it is born. It is called a joey. The joey drinks milk and grows in its mother's **pouch**. The joey's mother can hop very fast on her strong back legs.

BABY
KANGAROO

BABY GIRAFFE

A baby giraffe is called a calf. It is as tall as
a man. The calf can run a few hours after
it is born. Giraffes are the tallest animals in
the world.

Prairie dog pups are born in tunnels under the ground. After about six weeks, the pups crawl out of the tunnels. They hunt for insects and plants to eat. If danger is near, prairie dogs YIP, YIP, YIP to warn the others.

BABY

PRAIRIE DOG

BABY **BABOON**

A baby baboon rides on its mother's back as she looks for food. The baby learns which fruit and leaves are safe to eat. Baboons do not need to drink a lot of water. They get water from the food they eat.

A baby elephant stays close to its mother. It hides from danger under her legs. Big African elephants are sometimes killed by hunters. The hunters sell their **tusks**. Some elephants live in parks to stay safe from hunters.

ENDANGERED ANIMAL OF THE GRASSLANDS

BABY
AFRICAN
ELEPHANT

Learn More

Books

Jackson, Kay. *Explore the Grasslands.*
Mankato, Minn.: Capstone Press, 2006.

MacAulay, Kelley, and Bobbie Kalman. *A Grassland Habitat.* New York: Crabtree Pub. Co., 2006.

Rau, Dana Meachen. *The Lion in the Grass.*
New York: Marshall Cavendish Benchmark,
2006.

Web Sites

Enchanted Learning
© 2000–2007. *Biomes-Habitats.*
   http://www.enchantedlearning.com
   Click on "Biomes." Then click on "Grassland."

Missouri Botanical Garden
© 2005. *Biomes of the World.*
   http://www.mbgnet.net/

INDEX

~To our little Texans~Andrew, Charlie, and Kate~

Enslow Elementary, an imprint of Enslow Publishers, Inc.
Enslow Elementary® is a registered trademark of Enslow Publishers, Inc.

Copyright © 2009 by Carmen Bredeson

Library of Congress Cataloging-in-Publication Data

Bredeson, Carmen.
   Baby animals of the grasslands / Carmen Bredeson.
      p. cm. – (Nature's baby animals)
   Summary: "Up-close photos and information about baby animals of the grasslands biome"–Provided by publisher.
   Includes bibliographical references and index.
   ISBN-13: 978-0-7660-3006-0
   ISBN-10: 0-7660-3006-7
   1. Grassland animals–Infancy–Juvenile literature. I. Title.
   QL115.3.B74 2008
   591.74—dc22
                              2007029284

Printed in the United States of America

10 9 8 7 6 5 4 3 2 1

Note to Parents and Teachers: The Nature's Baby Animals series supports the National Science Education Standards for K–4 science. The Words to Know section introduces subject-specific vocabulary words, including pronunciation and definitions. Early readers may need help with these new words.

To Our Readers: We have done our best to make sure all Internet addresses in this book were active and appropriate when we went to press. However, the author and the publisher have no control over and assume no liability for the material available on those Internet sites or on other Web sites they may link to. Any comments or suggestions can be sent by e-mail to comments@enslow.com or to the address on the back cover.

Every effort has been made to locate all copyright holders of material used in this book. If any errors or omissions have occurred, corrections will be made in future editions of this book.

Enslow Publishers, Inc., is committed to printing our books on recycled paper. The paper in every book contains 10% to 30% post-consumer waste (PCW). The cover board on the outside of each book contains 100% PCW. Our goal is to do our part to help young people and the environment too!

Photo Credits: © 1999, Artville, LLC, p. 3; Animals Animals: © Barbara Von Hoffmann, p. 21, © D. Allen Photography, p. 19, © D&J Bartlett/OSF, p. 7, © Erwin & Peggy Bauer, p. 17, © Ingrid Van Den Berg, p. 6, © S. Michael Bisceglie, p. 10; © Manor Photography/Alamy, p. 16; Minden Pictures: © Mitsuaki Iwago, pp. 1, 8, © Richard Du Toit, p. 15, © Suzi Eszterhas, p. 11, © Yva Momatiuk/John Eastcott, p. 14; naturepl.com: © Dave Watts, p. 12, © Pete Oxford, pp. 13, 23, © Suzi Eszterhas, pp. 2 (left), 9; Shutterstock, p. 5; Visuals Unlimited: © Arthur Morris, p. 20, © Joe McDonald, pp. 2 (right), 18.

Cover Photo: © Mitsuaki Iwago/Minden Pictures

Enslow Elementary
an imprint of
Enslow Publishers, Inc.
40 Industrial Road
Box 398
Berkeley Heights, NJ 07922
USA
http://www.enslow.com